ROYAL HORTICULTURAL SOCIETY

DIARY 2025

FRANCES LINCOLN

RHS

First published in 2024 by Frances Lincoln Publishing, an imprint of The Quarto Group.
One Triptych Place, London, SE1 9SH
United Kingdom
www.Quarto.com

A catalogue record for this book is available from the British Library.

ISBN 978-0-7112-9182-9

10 9 8 7 6 5 4 3 2 1

Printed in China

RHS FLOWER SHOWS 2025

The Royal Horticultural Society holds a number of prestigious flower shows throughout the year. At the time of going to press, show dates for 2025 had not been confirmed but details can be found on the website at: rhs.org.uk/shows-events.

Every effort is made to ensure calendarial data is correct at the time of going to press but the publisher cannot accept any liability for any errors or changes.

Title page: Plate 4 – plants of the Linnaean class III – Triandria, detail.
Below and overleaf: Plate 12 – plants of the Linnaean class V – Pentandria, detail.

CALENDAR 2025

JANUARY

M	T	W	T	F	S	S
		1	2	3	4	5
6	7	8	9	10	11	12
13	14	15	16	17	18	19
20	21	22	23	24	25	26
27	28	29	30	31		

FEBRUARY

M	T	W	T	F	S	S
					1	2
3	4	5	6	7	8	9
10	11	12	13	14	15	16
17	18	19	20	21	22	23
24	25	26	27	28		

MARCH

M	T	W	T	F	S	S
					1	2
3	4	5	6	7	8	9
10	11	12	13	14	15	16
17	18	19	20	21	22	23
24	25	26	27	28	29	30
31						

APRIL

M	T	W	T	F	S	S
	1	2	3	4	5	6
7	8	9	10	11	12	13
14	15	16	17	18	19	20
21	22	23	24	25	26	27
28	29	30				

MAY

M	T	W	T	F	S	S
			1	2	3	4
5	6	7	8	9	10	11
12	13	14	15	16	17	18
19	20	21	22	23	24	25
26	27	28	29	30	31	

JUNE

M	T	W	T	F	S	S
						1
2	3	4	5	6	7	8
9	10	11	12	13	14	15
16	17	18	19	20	21	22
23	24	25	26	27	28	29
30						

JULY

M	T	W	T	F	S	S
	1	2	3	4	5	6
7	8	9	10	11	12	13
14	15	16	17	18	19	20
21	22	23	24	25	26	27
28	29	30	31			

AUGUST

M	T	W	T	F	S	S
				1	2	3
4	5	6	7	8	9	10
11	12	13	14	15	16	17
18	19	20	21	22	23	24
25	26	27	28	29	30	31

SEPTEMBER

M	T	W	T	F	S	S
1	2	3	4	5	6	7
8	9	10	11	12	13	14
15	16	17	18	19	20	21
22	23	24	25	26	27	28
29	30					

OCTOBER

M	T	W	T	F	S	S
		1	2	3	4	5
6	7	8	9	10	11	12
13	14	15	16	17	18	19
20	21	22	23	24	25	26
27	28	29	30	31		

NOVEMBER

M	T	W	T	F	S	S
					1	2
3	4	5	6	7	8	9
10	11	12	13	14	15	16
17	18	19	20	21	22	23
24	25	26	27	28	29	30

DECEMBER

M	T	W	T	F	S	S
1	2	3	4	5	6	7
8	9	10	11	12	13	14
15	16	17	18	19	20	21
22	23	24	25	26	27	28
29	30	31				

CALENDAR 2026

JANUARY

M	T	W	T	F	S	S
			1	2	3	4
5	6	7	8	9	10	11
12	13	14	15	16	17	18
19	20	21	22	23	24	25
26	27	28	29	30	31	

FEBRUARY

M	T	W	T	F	S	S
						1
2	3	4	5	6	7	8
9	10	11	12	13	14	15
16	17	18	19	20	21	22
23	24	25	26	27	28	

MARCH

M	T	W	T	F	S	S
						1
2	3	4	5	6	7	8
9	10	11	12	13	14	15
16	17	18	19	20	21	22
23	24	25	26	27	28	29
30	31					

APRIL

M	T	W	T	F	S	S
		1	2	3	4	5
6	7	8	9	10	11	12
13	14	15	16	17	18	19
20	21	22	23	24	25	26
27	28	29	30			

MAY

M	T	W	T	F	S	S
				1	2	3
4	5	6	7	8	9	10
11	12	13	14	15	16	17
18	19	20	21	22	23	24
25	26	27	28	29	30	31

JUNE

M	T	W	T	F	S	S
1	2	3	4	5	6	7
8	9	10	11	12	13	14
15	16	17	18	19	20	21
22	23	24	25	26	27	28
29	30					

JULY

M	T	W	T	F	S	S
		1	2	3	4	5
6	7	8	9	10	11	12
13	14	15	16	17	18	19
20	21	22	23	24	25	26
27	28	29	30	31		

AUGUST

M	T	W	T	F	S	S
					1	2
3	4	5	6	7	8	9
10	11	12	13	14	15	16
17	18	19	20	21	22	23
24	25	26	27	28	29	30
31						

SEPTEMBER

M	T	W	T	F	S	S
1	2	3	4	5	6	
7	8	9	10	11	12	13
14	15	16	17	18	19	20
21	22	23	24	25	26	27
28	29	30				

OCTOBER

M	T	W	T	F	S	S
			1	2	3	4
5	6	7	8	9	10	11
12	13	14	15	16	17	18
19	20	21	22	23	24	25
26	27	28	29	30	31	

NOVEMBER

M	T	W	T	F	S	S
						1
2	3	4	5	6	7	8
9	10	11	12	13	14	15
16	17	18	19	20	21	22
23	24	25	26	27	28	29
30						

DECEMBER

M	T	W	T	F	S	S
	1	2	3	4	5	6
7	8	9	10	11	12	13
14	15	16	17	18	19	20
21	22	23	24	25	26	27
28	29	30	31			

CHRISTIAN GOTTLIEB GEISSLER (1729–1814)

Tabulae phytographicae by Johannes Gessner (1709–90) is a work of stunning beauty. The book was more than a lavish visual feast, though. It was a work of scientific value and an educational tool for the development of botanical study, for which its illustrations were central.

Gessner, a Swiss botanist, was greatly influenced by the writings of Carl Linnaeus (1707–78) and his sexual system for classification, in which he saw 'what a desired reformation they brought about in botany and natural history, and how much the study would gain in brilliancy, completeness and finish' if Linnaean taxonomy was followed more widely. Gessner determined to compile a comprehensive history of plants with text and plates illustrating Linnaeus' system, allowing users to visualise different classes of plants, their arrangement and features. Gessner hoped this would aid the ready adoption of Linnaean principles, encouraging botanical learning and research.

Gessner intended the work's illustrations to be clear and accessible. He commissioned the German-Swiss artist Christian Gottlieb Geissler (1729–1814) to assist as draughtsman and engraver. Geissler specialised in natural history subjects, though initially trained as a miniaturist. He was therefore particularly suited to capturing and arranging the detailed images that Gessner envisaged.

Geissler moved into Gessner's household in the 1750s to undertake the project, where his skills would be tested. He was required to lay out the plates as composites, tabulating over 1000 plants (illustrated from live or dried specimens or adapted from other published sources) in an arrangement that showcased the reproductive components useful for classification. The talent of the miniaturist was crucial to adapt the images to fit as a grouping without loss of detail. Composite plates were ideal for comparative study, but also reduced the number of costly plates required for the work, as Gessner was keen to ensure that the book would be affordable for potential purchasers.

Linnaeus, with whom Gessner had been in correspondence since the 1740s, received preliminary plates in 1763 for his approval. His response captures their magnificence:

'When I saw your plates ... as beautiful as they are fine, suitable and select, I was thunderstruck ... I embrace you in my arms, I kiss you; if any trifles lie in my power, by Flora and her flowers, I entreat you to let me know.'

Gessner and Linnaeus would not live to see the book's publication, it being brought to print in 1795 under the title *Tabulae phytographicae* by Gessner's relative, Christoph Salomon Schinz (1764–1847). Geissler left a botanical legacy through his contributions, cementing his reputation. He would go on to found a school in Geneva, training the next generation of artists and engravers, while *Tabluae phytographicae* became a valuable resource for students and professionals alike, as well as connoisseurs of botanical illustration.

Jessica Hudson
RHS Rare Books Librarian

References from de Beer, G.R. (1949). The Correspondence between Linnaeus and Johann Gesner. *Proceedings Linnean Society London*, Vol. 161 (2), p. 229.

Elliott, B. (2008). Botanical Art in the Age of Linnaeus. *The Linnean*, Special Issue No. 8, pp. 97–106.

Knittel, M. (2022). Flora Near and Far: Accumulating Knowledge on Plants in Eighteenth-Century Zurich in *Connecting Territories Exploring People and Nature, 1700–1850. Emergence of Natural History*, Vol. 5, pp. 75–100.

Knittel, M. (2017). Beobachten, ordnen, erklären: Johannes Gessners Tabulae phytographicae (1795–1804) in Vuillemin, N. & Dueck, E. (eds.) *Entre l'oeil et le monde Dispositifs d'une nouvelle épistémologie visuelle dans les sciences de la nature (1740–1840)*. Épistémocritique, pp. 33–45.

30 Monday

31 Tuesday

01 Wednesday

New Year's Day
Holiday, UK, Republic of Ireland, USA, Canada,
Australia and New Zealand

02 Thursday

Holiday, Scotland and New Zealand

03 Friday

04 Saturday

05 Sunday

Plate 12 – plants of the Linnaean class V – Pentandria, detail.

First quarter
Epiphany

Monday 06

Tuesday 07

Wednesday 08

Thursday 09

Friday 10

Saturday 11

Sunday 12

Plate 2 – plants of the Linnaean class II – Diandria, detail.

JANUARY

13 Monday

Full moon

14 Tuesday

15 Wednesday

16 Thursday

17 Friday

18 Saturday

19 Sunday

Plate 2 – plants of the Linnaean class II – Diandria, detail.

JANUARY

Martin Luther King Jnr Day
Holiday, USA

Monday 20

Last quarter

Tuesday 21

Wednesday 22

Thursday 23

Friday 24

Burns Night

Saturday 25

Australia Day

Sunday 26

Plate 3 – plants of the Linnaean class II – Diandria, detail.

JANUARY–FEBRUARY

27 Monday

Holiday, Australia (Australia Day)

28 Tuesday

29 Wednesday

New moon
Chinese New Year

30 Thursday

31 Friday

01 Saturday

02 Sunday

Plate 3 – plants of the Linnaean class II – Diandria, detail.

FEBRUARY

Monday 03

Tuesday 04

First quarter

Wednesday 05

Waitangi Day
Holiday, New Zealand

Thursday 06

Friday 07

Saturday 08

Sunday 09

Plate 4 – plants of the Linnaean class III – Triandria, detail.

10 Monday

11 Tuesday

12 Wednesday

Full moon

13 Thursday

14 Friday

Valentine's Day

15 Saturday

16 Sunday

Plate 5 – plants of the Linnaean class III – Triandria, detail.

FEBRUARY

Presidents' Day
Holiday, USA

Monday 17

Tuesday 18

Wednesday 19

Last quarter

Thursday 20

Friday 21

Saturday 22

Sunday 23

Plate 5 – plants of the Linnaean class III – Triandria, detail.

24 Monday

25 Tuesday

26 Wednesday

27 Thursday

28 Friday   *New moon*

01 Saturday   St David's Day
First day of Ramadân (subject to sighting of the moon)

02 Sunday

Plate 8 – plants of the Linnaean class IV – Tetrandria, detail.

MARCH

Monday 03

Shrove Tuesday

Tuesday 04

Ash Wednesday

Wednesday 05

First quarter

Thursday 06

Friday 07

Saturday 08

Sunday 09

Plate 9 – plants of the Linnaean class IV – Tetrandria, detail.

10 Monday   Commonwealth Day

---

11 Tuesday

---

12 Wednesday

---

13 Thursday

---

14 Friday   *Full moon*

---

15 Saturday

---

16 Sunday

Plate 9 – plants of the Linnaean class IV – Tetrandria, detail.

MARCH

St Patrick's Day
Holiday, Republic of Ireland and Northern Ireland

Monday 17

Tuesday 18

Wednesday 19

Vernal Equinox (Spring begins)

Thursday 20

Friday 21

Last quarter

Saturday 22

Sunday 23

Plate 10 – plants of the Linnaean class IV – Tetrandria, detail.

24 Monday

25 Tuesday

26 Wednesday

27 Thursday

28 Friday

29 Saturday

New moon

30 Sunday

British Summer Time begins
Mothering Sunday, UK and Republic of Ireland
Eid al-Fitr (end of Ramadân) (subject to sighting of the moon)

Plate 11 – plants of the Linnaean class V – Pentandria, detail.

MARCH–APRIL

Monday 31

Tuesday 01

Wednesday 02

Thursday 03

Friday 04

First quarter

Saturday 05

Sunday 06

Plate 11 – plants of the Linnaean class V – Pentandria, detail.

APRIL

07 Monday

08 Tuesday

09 Wednesday

10 Thursday

11 Friday

12 Saturday

13 Sunday

Full moon
Palm Sunday
First day of Passover (Pesach)

Plate 13 – plants of the Linnaean class V – Pentandria, detail.

APRIL

Monday 14

Tuesday 15

Wednesday 16

Maundy Thursday

Thursday 17

Good Friday
Holiday, UK, Canada, Australia and New Zealand

Friday 18

Saturday 19

Easter Sunday

Sunday 20

Plate 14 – plants of the Linnaean class V – Pentandria, detail.

APRIL

21 Monday

Last quarter
Easter Monday
Holiday, UK (exc. Scotland), Republic of Ireland,
Australia and New Zealand

22 Tuesday

Earth Day

23 Wednesday

St George's Day

24 Thursday

25 Friday

Anzac Day
Holiday, Australia and New Zealand

26 Saturday

27 Sunday

New moon

Plate 15 – plants of the Linnaean class V – Pentandria, detail.

APRIL–MAY

Monday 28

Tuesday 29

Wednesday 30

Thursday 01

Friday 02

Saturday 03

First quarter   Sunday 04

Plate 15 – plants of the Linnaean class V – Pentandria, detail.

MAY

05 Monday

Early Spring Bank Holiday, UK
Holiday, Republic of Ireland

06 Tuesday

Coronation Day

07 Wednesday

08 Thursday

09 Friday

10 Saturday

11 Sunday

Mother's Day, USA, Canada,
Australia and New Zealand

Plate 16 – plants of the Linnaean class V – Pentandria, detail.

Full moon Monday 12

Tuesday 13

Wednesday 14

Thursday 15

Friday 16

Saturday 17

Sunday 18

Plate 16 – plants of the Linnaean class V – Pentandria, detail.

MAY

---

19 Monday

Victoria Day
Holiday, Canada

---

20 Tuesday

Last quarter

---

21 Wednesday

---

22 Thursday

---

23 Friday

---

24 Saturday

---

25 Sunday

Plate 17 – plants of the Linnaean class VI – Hexandria, detail.

MAY–JUNE

Spring Bank Holiday, UK
Memorial Day
Holiday, USA

Monday 26

New moon

Tuesday 27

Wednesday 28

Ascension Day

Thursday 29

Friday 30

Saturday 31

Sunday 01

Plate 17 – plants of the Linnaean class VI – Hexandria, detail.

JUNE

---

02 Monday

Feast of Weeks (Shavuot)
Holiday, Republic of Ireland
Holiday, New Zealand (The King's Birthday)

---

03 Tuesday

First quarter

---

04 Wednesday

---

05 Thursday

---

06 Friday

---

07 Saturday

First day of Eid al-Adha

---

08 Sunday

Whit Sunday

Plate 18 – plants of the Linnaean class V – Pentandria, detail.

JUNE

Holiday, Australia (The King's Birthday)   **Monday 09**

Tuesday 10

Full moon   **Wednesday 11**

Thursday 12

Friday 13

The King's Official Birthday (subject to confirmation)   **Saturday 14**

Father's Day, UK, Republic of Ireland, USA and Canada
Trinity Sunday   **Sunday 15**

Plate 18 – plants of the Linnaean class V – Pentandria, detail.

JUNE

16 Monday

17 Tuesday

18 Wednesday   *Last quarter*

19 Thursday   Juneteenth
                                                           Holiday, USA
                                                         Corpus Christi

20 Friday   Holiday, New Zealand (Matariki)

21 Saturday   Summer solstice (Summer begins)

22 Sunday

Plate 19 – plants of the Linnaean class V – Pentandria, detail.

JUNE

Monday 23

Tuesday 24

New moon   Wednesday 25

Thursday 26

Islamic New Year   Friday 27

Saturday 28

Sunday 29

Plate 20 – plants of the Linnaean class V – Pentandria, detail.

30 Monday

01 Tuesday

Canada Day
Holiday, Canada

02 Wednesday

First quarter

03 Thursday

04 Friday

Independence Day
Holiday, USA

05 Saturday

06 Sunday

Plate 21 – plants of the Linnaean class V – Pentandria, detail.

JULY

Monday 07

Tuesday 08

Wednesday 09

Full moon   Thursday 10

Friday 11

Battle of the Boyne   Saturday 12

Sunday 13

Plate 21 – plants of the Linnaean class V – Pentandria, detail.

JULY

14 Monday — Holiday, Northern Ireland (Battle of the Boyne)

15 Tuesday — St Swithin's Day

16 Wednesday

17 Thursday

18 Friday — *Last quarter*

19 Saturday

20 Sunday

Plate 22 – plants of the Linnaean class VI – Hexandria, detail.

JULY

Monday 21

Tuesday 22

Wednesday 23

New moon   Thursday 24

Friday 25

Saturday 26

Sunday 27

Plate 22 – plants of the Linnaean class VI – Hexandria, detail.

28 Monday

29 Tuesday

30 Wednesday

31 Thursday

01 Friday   *First quarter*

02 Saturday

03 Sunday

Plate 1 – plants of the Linnaean class I – Monandria, detail.

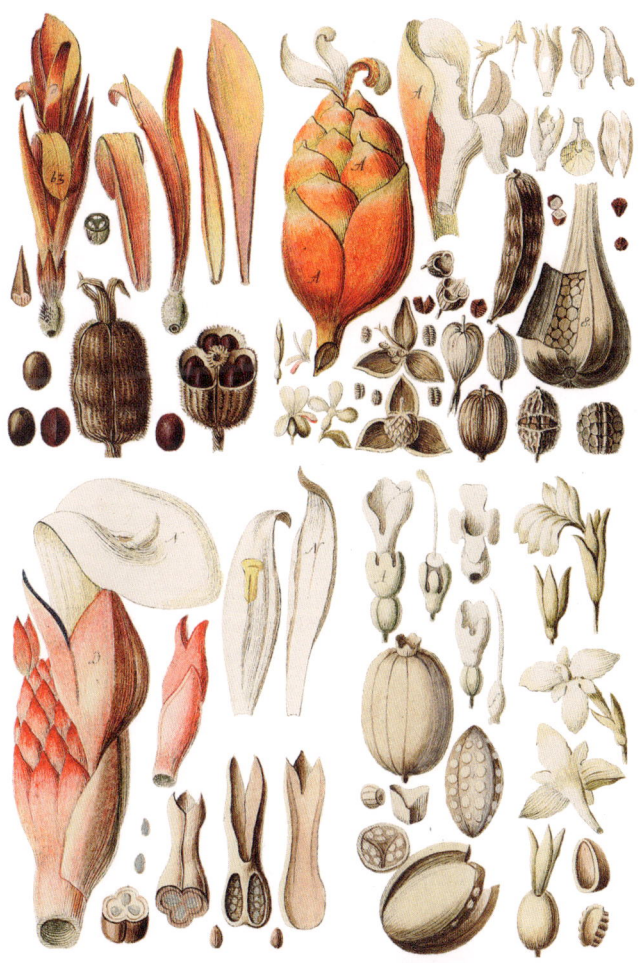

AUGUST

Holiday, Scotland and Republic of Ireland

Monday 04

Tuesday 05

Wednesday 06

Thursday 07

Friday 08

Full moon

Saturday 09

Sunday 10

Plate 7 – plants of the Linnaean class III – Triandria, detail.

AUGUST

11 Monday

12 Tuesday

13 Wednesday

14 Thursday

15 Friday

16 Saturday   *Last quarter*

17 Sunday

Plate 23 – plants of the Linnaean class V – Pentandria, detail.

AUGUST

Monday 18

Tuesday 19

Wednesday 20

Thursday 21

Friday 22

New moon   Saturday 23

Sunday 24

Plate 23 – plants of the Linnaean class V – Pentandria, detail.

AUGUST

25 Monday   Summer Bank Holiday, UK (exc. Scotland)

---

26 Tuesday

---

27 Wednesday

---

28 Thursday

---

29 Friday

---

30 Saturday

---

31 Sunday   *First quarter*

Plate 24 – plants of the Linnaean class VI – Hexandria, detail.

SEPTEMBER

Holiday, USA (Labor Day)   Monday 01
Holiday, Canada (Labour Day)

                                                             Tuesday 02

                                                          Wednesday 03

                                                           Thursday 04

                                                              Friday 05

                                                           Saturday 06

Full moon   Sunday 07
Father's Day, Australia and New Zealand

Plate 26 – plants of the Linnaean class VII – Heptandria, detail.

SEPTEMBER

08 Monday   Accession of King Charles III

09 Tuesday

10 Wednesday

11 Thursday

12 Friday

13 Saturday

14 Sunday   *Last quarter*

Plate 26 – plants of the Linnaean class VII – Heptandria, detail.

SEPTEMBER

Monday 15

Tuesday 16

Wednesday 17

Thursday 18

Friday 19

Saturday 20

New moon   Sunday 21

Plate 27 – plants of the Linnaean class IX – Enneandria, detail.

SEPTEMBER

22 Monday   Autumnal Equinox (Autumn begins)

23 Tuesday   Jewish New Year (Rosh Hashanah)

24 Wednesday

25 Thursday

26 Friday

27 Saturday

28 Sunday

Plate 27 – plants of the Linnaean class IX – Enneandria, detail.

SEPTEMBER–OCTOBER

First quarter
Michaelmas Day

Monday 29

Tuesday 30

Wednesday 01

Day of Atonement (Yom Kippur)

Thursday 02

Friday 03

Saturday 04

Sunday 05

Plate 28 – plants of the Linnaean class X – Decandria, detail.

OCTOBER

06 Monday

07 Tuesday

Full moon
First day of Tabernacles (Succoth)

08 Wednesday

09 Thursday

10 Friday

11 Saturday

12 Sunday

Plate 29 – plants of the Linnaean class X – Decandria, detail.

OCTOBER

Last quarter
Holiday, USA (Columbus Day)
Holiday, Canada (Thanksgiving)

Monday 13

Tuesday 14

Wednesday 15

Thursday 16

Friday 17

Saturday 18

Sunday 19

Plate 29 – plants of the Linnaean class X – Decandria, detail.

OCTOBER

20 Monday

21 Tuesday *New moon*

22 Wednesday

23 Thursday

24 Friday

25 Saturday

26 Sunday British Summer Time ends

Plate 30 – plants of the Linnaean class X – Decandria, detail.

OCTOBER–NOVEMBER

Holiday, Republic of Ireland
Holiday, New Zealand (Labour Day)

Monday 27

Tuesday 28

First quarter

Wednesday 29

Thursday 30

Halloween

Friday 31

All Saints' Day

Saturday 01

Sunday 02

Plate 30 – plants of the Linnaean class X – Decandria, detail.

NOVEMBER

03 Monday

04 Tuesday

05 Wednesday

Full moon
Guy Fawkes Night

06 Thursday

07 Friday

08 Saturday

09 Sunday

Remembrance Sunday

Plate 31 – plants of the Linnaean class X – Decandria, detail.

NOVEMBER

Monday 10

Holiday, USA (Veterans Day)
Holiday, Canada (Remembrance Day)

Tuesday 11

Last quarter

Wednesday 12

Thursday 13

Birthday of King Charles III

Friday 14

Saturday 15

Sunday 16

Plate 31 – plants of the Linnaean class X – Decandria, detail.

NOVEMBER

17 Monday

18 Tuesday

19 Wednesday

20 Thursday   *New moon*

21 Friday

22 Saturday

23 Sunday

Plate 32 – plants of the Linnaean class XII – Icosandria, detail.

NOVEMBER

Monday 24

Tuesday 25

Wednesday 26

Holiday, USA (Thanksgiving)   Thursday 27

First quarter   Friday 28

Saturday 29

St Andrew's Day   Sunday 30
First Sunday in Advent

Plate 32 – plants of the Linnaean class XII – Icosandria, detail.

DECEMBER

01 Monday   Holiday, Scotland (St Andrew's Day)

02 Tuesday

03 Wednesday

04 Thursday   *Full moon*

05 Friday

06 Saturday

07 Sunday

Plate 33 – plants of the Linnaean class XII – Icosandria, detail.

DECEMBER

Monday 08

Tuesday 09

Wednesday 10

Last quarter   Thursday 11

Friday 12

Saturday 13

Hanukkah begins (at sunset)   **Sunday 14**

Plate 34 – plants of the Linnaean class XII – Icosandria, detail.

DECEMBER

15 Monday

16 Tuesday

17 Wednesday

18 Thursday

19 Friday

20 Saturday   *New moon*

21 Sunday   Winter Solstice (Winter begins)

Plate 35 – plants of the Linnaean class XIII – Polyandria, detail.

DECEMBER

Hanukkah ends

Monday 22

Tuesday 23

Christmas Eve

Wednesday 24

Christmas Day
Holiday, UK, Republic of Ireland, USA,
Canada, Australia and New Zealand

Thursday 25

Boxing Day (St Stephen's Day)
Holiday, UK, Republic of Ireland, USA,
Canada, Australia and New Zealand

Friday 26

First quarter

Saturday 27

Sunday 28

Plate 35 – plants of the Linnaean class XIII – Polyandria, detail.

DECEMBER–JANUARY

29 Monday

30 Tuesday

31 Wednesday   New Year's Eve

01 Thursday   New Year's Day
                                          Holiday, UK, Republic of Ireland, USA,
                                            Canada, Australia and New Zealand

02 Friday   Holiday, Scotland and New Zealand

03 Saturday

04 Sunday

Plate 37 – plants of the Linnaean class XIII – Polyandria, detail.

YEAR PLANNER

January	July
February	August
March	September
April	October
May	November
June	December